WELSHPOOL
TO LLANFAIR

Vic Mitchell and Keith Smith

MP Middleton Press

Front cover: **The Earl** *and* **The Countess** *were built for the opening of the line and operated it exclusively for more than 50 years. The latter is seen at the end of the line at Welshpool on 4th May 2002. (M.J.Stretton)*

Back cover: **The Earl** *stands in front of* **Countess** *outside their new home at Llanfair Caereinion in June 2003. When the GWR took over, the latter's nameplate was shortened from* **The Countess** *to* **Countess** *to make it fit the cab side. In 1962, it became* **The Countess** *again but it reverted to* **Countess** *in 1995. (P.Jones)*

Published April 2009

ISBN 978 1 906008 49 9

© Middleton Press, 2009

Design Deborah Esher
Typesetting Barbara Mitchell

Published by
       Middleton Press
       Easebourne Lane
       Midhurst
       West Sussex
       GU29 9AZ
Tel: 01730 813169
Fax: 01730 812601
Email: info@middletonpress.co.uk
www.middletonpress.co.uk

Printed in the United Kingdom by Henry Ling Limited, at the Dorset Press, Dorchester, DT1 1HD

CONTENTS

ACKNOWLEDGEMENTS

We are very grateful for the assistance received from many of those mentioned in the credits also to P.A.Bailey, A.R.Carder, L.Crosier, G.Croughton, D.A.Johnson, D.K.Jones, M.D.Lister, N.Langridge, B.Lewis, D.H.Mitchell, Mr D.Salter and Dr S.Salter, G.T.V.Stacey, E.Wilmshurst and in particular, our always supportive wives, Barbara Mitchell and Janet Smith.

INTRODUCTION

Late into the railway scene, this 20th century railway backwater lasted only a little over 50 years, but less than 30 for passengers.

The pioneers in railway preservation were concerned with the Talyllyn and Festiniog on the Welsh coast. Thus many had to travel through Welshpool regularly to reach the object of their passion.

I was one of those who went round the roundabout at Raven Square more than once at about 3.0am en route from London to the FR on many Saturdays in the mid-1950s. Too exhausted to take any interest in the W&LLR on the return, we had to leave the welfare of this unique item of Welsh heritage to many of those who lived nearer.

The acquisition of the line was more protracted and difficult than that of the FR, but the eventual result has been the creation of an equally polished and professional enterprise, with a diverse range of rolling stock.

Sadly lost for ever was the line through the streets of Welshpool, which fascinated all, but were visited by only a few and so a large part of this album is devoted to this unusual and long lost byway.

Vic Mitchell

I. Pre-1931 route map. (Railway Magazine)

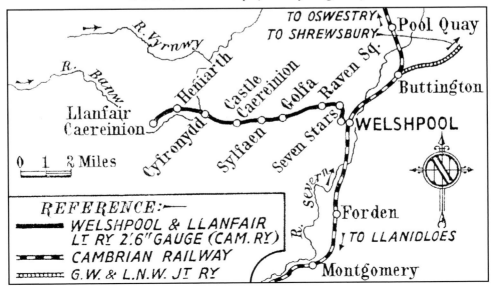

GEOGRAPHICAL SETTING

Welshpool developed on the west bank of the River Severn and became an important market and commercial centre. The line west to Llanfair Caereinion was built on undulating agricultural land, overlying limestones and shales of little commercial value, although there was one quarry at Raven Square.

The route follows the Sylfaen Brook upstream and near the middle part of the line it passes over the watershed. Thereafter it drops into the valley of the River Banwy near Cyfronydd. This flows through the centre of Llanfair, which had a market on the first Friday of every month.

The route was constructed entirely within the county of Montgomeryshire, now part of Powys.

North is at the top of the maps, but not necessarily the diagrams.

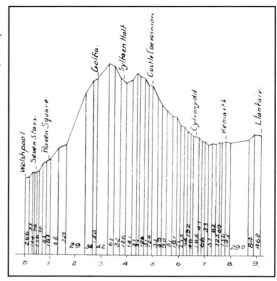

GWR Gradient Profile →

HISTORICAL BACKGROUND

Main line trains arrived in Welshpool from Oswestry in 1860 and continued south in 1861. They were operated by Cambrian Railways from 1864.

The Welshpool & Llanfair Light Railway was authorised in 1899, under the 1896 Light Railways Act, and arrangements were made for it to be operated by the CR. The gauge chosen was 2ft 6ins, rare in the UK. It opened to goods traffic on 9th March 1903 and to passengers on 4th April of that year.

The CR and the W&LLR became part of the Great Western Railway in 1922-23 and this formed the Western Region of British Railways upon nationalisation in 1948. However, passenger service to Llanfair had been withdrawn on 7th February 1931. Freight withdrawal came on 5th November 1956 and a preservation society was formed later that month.

A company was eventually created and a Light Railway Order was obtained in 1962, a lease having been obtained that year. Both excluded the track in the urban part of Welshpool.

Reopening between Llanfair and Castle Caereinion took place on 6th April 1963. Trains ran to Sylfaen in the Summer of 1964, but not regularly until 15th July 1972. Completion to Welshpool (Raven Square) was achieved on 8th July 1981.

II. The 1ins to 1 mile map is from 1921.

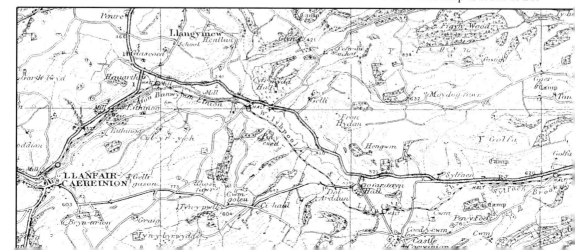

A GWR 19-seater 25hp Thornycroft was photographed in July 1928 in The Square in Llanfair Caereinion. The Lion Hotel later became the Red Lion. The bus is working the connection to Dinas Mawddwy, which received GWR passenger trains until 1930. The branch is featured in our *Newtown to Aberystwyth* album. (GWR)

Locomotives

Name	No.	Builder	Type	Built	Previous Workplace	Year of arrival
The Earl	1	Beyer Peacock	0-6-0T	1902	-	1902
The Countess	2	Beyer Peacock	0-6-0T	1902	-	1902
Nutty	5	Sentinel	0-4-0-VB	1929	Fletton Brickworks	1964 *
Monarch	6	Bagnall	0-4-4-0T	1953	Sittingbourne	1966
Chattenden	7	Drewry	0-6-0DM	1949	Admiralty Depots	1968
Dougal	8	Barclay	0-4-0T	1946	Provan Gasworks	1969
Sir Drefaldwyn	10	S.F.Belge	0-8-0T	1944	Austria	1969
Ferret	11	Hunslet	0-4-0DM	1940	Admiralty Depots	1971
Joan	12	Kerr Stuart	0-6-2T	1927	Antigua	1971
SLR No. 85	14	Hunslet	2-6-2T	1954	Sierra Leone	1975
Orion	15	Tubize	2-6-2T	1948	Finland	1983 *
Scooby	16	Hunslet	0-4-0DM	1941	Admiralty Depots	1992
TSC No. 175	17	Diema	0-6-0DM	1978	Taiwan	2004
CFI 764.423	18	Resita	0-8-0T	1954	Romania	2008
CFI 764.425	19	Resita	0-8-0T	1954	Romania	2007

* Subsequently sold   Nos 3, 4 and 9 were temporary diesel shunters

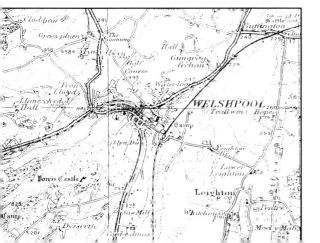

Coaches

2	Replica W&L Pickering coaches
1	Replica Zillertalbahn coach
5	Zillertalbahn coaches
1	Saltzkammergut Lokalbahn
3	Sierra Leone coaches
2	Hungarian State Railway coaches

PASSENGER SERVICES

These notes refer to the pre-1931 weekday service; no Sunday trains were on record. Trains running on every weekday numbered four for most of the Cambrian years of the line, with an extra one on certain days.

However, the basic frequency was reduced to three by the GWR and from 1925 it also offered a bus service. The bus took only 33 minutes for the journey.

In 1930 the GWR road services were renamed "Western Transport" and from 1933 were operated by Crosville Motor Services Ltd.

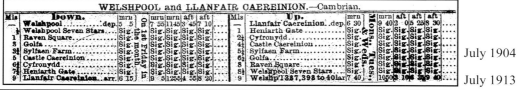

July 1904

July 1913

WELSHPOOL and LLANFAIR CAEREINION.—Cambrian.

NOTES.

‡ Runs 20 minutes *earlier* on the 1st Friday in the month.
t Runs on Thursdays, Saturdays, and Llanfair Fair Days only.

WELSHPOOL and LLANFAIR CAEREINION.—G. W. (late Cambrian).

A Runs on the 1st and 3rd Monday.   Z Stop when required.
¶ "Halt" at Sylfaen between Golfa and Castle Caereinion.

June 1922

November 1930

WELSHPOOL and LLANFAIR CAEREINION.

Aa Stop when required.   B1 Except Mondays.   M Mondays only.

September 1925

WELSHPOOL and LLANFAIR CAEREINION.—Great Western (late Cambrian).

Aa Stop when required.   B1 Except Mondays.   M Mondays only.
R Tuesdays, Wednesdays, and Saturdays.   T Runs on 1st and 3rd Mondays.

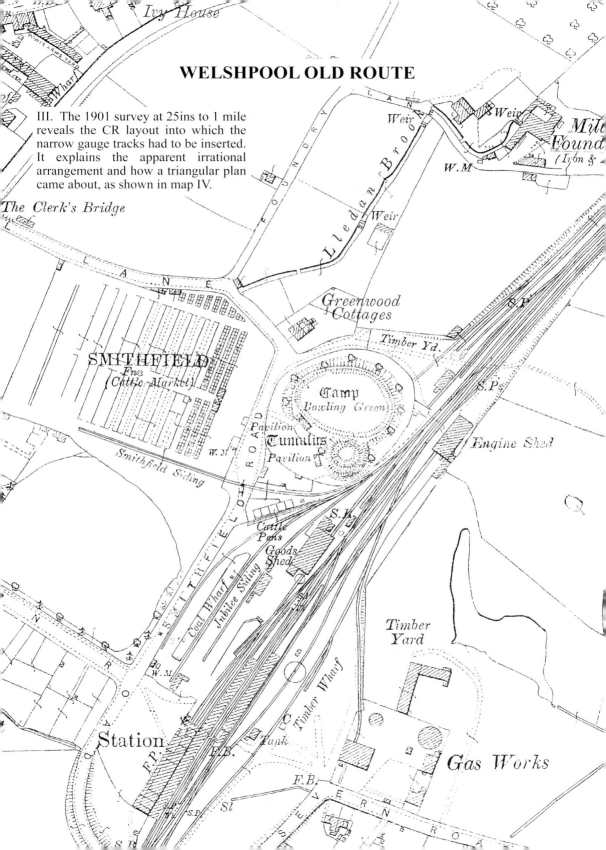

WELSHPOOL OLD ROUTE

III. The 1901 survey at 25ins to 1 mile reveals the CR layout into which the narrow gauge tracks had to be inserted. It explains the apparent irrational arrangement and how a triangular plan came about, as shown in map IV.

Ivy House

The Clerk's Bridge

Weir

Weir

Weir

W.M

Mill Found (Iron &

Lledan Brook

FOUNDRY LANE

Greenwood Cottages

Timber Yd.

S.P.

LANE

SMITHFIELD Fn⚫ (Cattle Market)

Camp Bowling Green

S.P.

Smithfield Siding

W.M

Pavilion

Tumulus

Pavilion

Engine Shed

SMITHFIELD ROAD

Cattle Pens

Goods Shed

S.B.

Coal Wharf

Jubilee Siding

Timber Wharf

Timber Yard

S.P.

Station

F.P.

F.B.

Tank

C Timber Wharf

W.M

S.B.

NEWTON ROAD

Gas Works

F.B.

S.P.

S

SEVERN ROAD

Old Quarries
Ceunant Cottage

490

Stepping Stones

Bron-y-Buckley Wood

Ceunant

Armory

BROOK STREET

Lodge

F Bs

MOUNT ST

HIGH ST

RAVEN STREET

Raven Bridge

Sch

Christ Church

WELSHPOOL

(Trallwm)

Maes Gwastad

Llyn-du Ditch

Llyn-du Cottage

Oldford

Traeth

Lloyd's Bank

Old Quarry

IV.   The 1949 survey is shown at 12ins to 1 mile, having been doubled from its published scale. The present terminus is near the left border. The OS made very few errors, but the route west of Church Street is wrong. It is shown correctly on map VI, near photograph 36. The surveyors sometimes omitted tracks at this scale and so the loop and the sidings to the sheds are not present, but the photographs clarify their positions.

Reservoir

Myrtle Villa *Maes-y-gareg*

GUNGROG

WATERLOO

Westwood

School

Trafalgar House

Weir

Hospl

GUNGROG

Clinic

DOCK

Lledan

Mill Lane Foundry

SP

Vic

Lledan Brook

The Clerk's Bridge

MILL LANE

GREENFIELDS

Weirs

SP

HUTCH ST

SEVERN ST

Motte & Bailey

SP

Engine Shed

SEVERN RD

Gas Works

W

W

Elmhurst

Sta

SP

County Intermediate School

MP

Severn Cottage

The Terminus

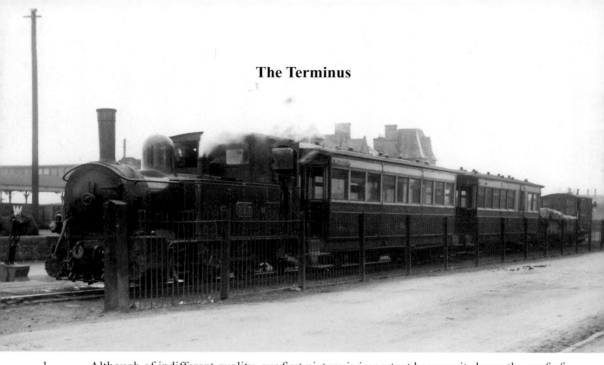

1.　　　Although of indifferent quality, our first picture is important because it shows the roof of the former Cambrian Railways station building located on the up platform of the main line station and thus provides orientation for the starting point of the narrow gauge. (P.Q.Treloar coll.)

2.　　　No. 823 *Countess* leaves the terminus with the 8.10am mixed train to Llanfair on 6th April 1926. All the narrow gauge points on the running line were worked and locked by ground frames. No.1 ground frame (2 levers) is seen on the left of the photograph and operated the points which provided access to the transhipment shed. (K.Nunn/LCGB)

3.   *Countess* is at the coal stage and a GWR standard gauge open wagon stands the other side of it. The platform for loading livestock onto standard gauge wagons can be seen in the right background. (P.Q.Treloar coll.)

4.   The cab of *The Earl* is in front of the engine shed, while the chimney is in line with the carriage shed. The chimneys seen in pictures 1 to 4 were replaced by the GWR with their copper cap type. (P.Chancellor coll.)

5.   This undated scene shows the prospective passengers perspective and the merits of plus fours attire. The coach was always at the front of the train so that its vacuum brakes could be connected to the locomotive. (P.Q.Treloar coll.)

For photographs of the main line, please see pictures 64 to 72 in our *Shrewsbury to Newtown* album.

6.   When photographed in 1946, the two sheds had lost the 'whiteness' of their asbestos cladding. The main line standard gauge goods shed is in the centre background, with the transhipment shed containing both a narrow gauge and a standard gauge track to its right. (E.Johnson)

7.   Looking in the opposite direction from the previous photograph, but in the same position beside the loco shed, we can see part of Welshpool town and St. Mary's Church in the background. The line ran close to the church. (E.Johnson)

8.   A view in the same direction as picture no. 1 includes the station footbridge and the former ticket office for the Llanfair line passengers. It is to the right of the locomotive cab and is seen on 17th May 1956. The first station was in the road to the right of the railings. (H.Davies)

9.   The three original coaches were disposed of in the 1930s and so open wagons with benches from the main line station platforms and waiting rooms were used to provide seating accommodation on the special trains which operated between 1949 and closure in 1956. (P.Q.Treloar coll.)

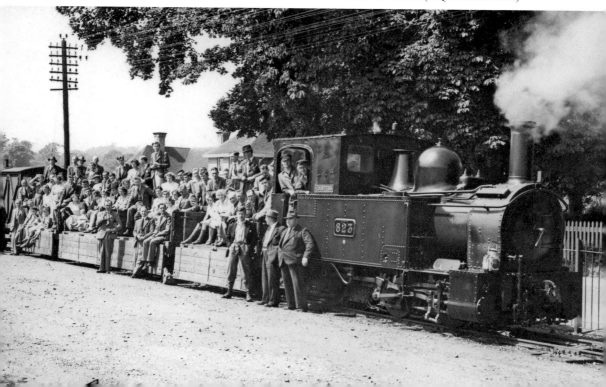

10.   This undated profile of *The Earl* was recorded outside the locomotive shed. The tapered safety valve cover was a GWR feature, as was steam heating for the coaches. The carriage shed had been fitted with new doors. (P.Q.Treloar coll.)

11.   *The Earl* crosses Smithfield Road on 24th August 1948. Many cars then had wooden bodies; this one was registered in Manchester in 1936. (H.C.Casserley)

12.   *Countess* has assembled its train and is ready to leave the yard on 11th May 1949. The dock siding is standard gauge. Trains usually ran on Mondays at 7.30am, as it was market day in Welshpool. The 11.30 ran every weekday, apart from Wednesdays and Saturdays. (M.Whitehouse coll.)

13.　　Smartly prepared, *The Earl* was recorded on a farm equipment sale day, but the date was not noted. (L.M.Hobdey/J.M.Bentley coll.)

14.　　The motive power fleet is lined up outside the carriage shed on 9th July 1949. Normally the locomotives alternated every two weeks. *Countess* is nearer the camera with *The Earl* behind. (R.S.Carpenter coll.)

15.   It is sale day in the livestock market as coal is shovelled from a 10-ton standard gauge wagon onto the coal stage for the benefit of *The Earl*. The locomotive nameplates had been removed by this time. (L.M.Hobdey/J.M.Bentley coll.)

CAMBRIAN RAILWAYS,
Issued subject to the conditions
stated on the Co's Time Tables.

WELSHPOOL To
GOLFA
THIRD CLASS (PARLY)   FARE -/3

Welshpool   Welshpool
Golfa   Golfa

Gt Western Ry   Western Ry
LLANFAIR   LLANFAIR
CAEREINION   CAEREINION
WELSHPOOL
3RD CLASS
Fare 7d
issued subject to the conditions & regulations set
out in the Company's Time Tables Bills & Notices
WELSHPOOL   WELSHPOOL

3542   3542

16.   No. 822 returns from Llanfair and crosses Smithfield Road. The photograph gives us the opportunity to see the transhipment shed and the wagons of different dimensions therein. (A.W.V.Mace/Milepost 92½)

17.   No. 822 is seen again with the goods shed to the left of it. The cattle loading ramp is on the left and the track to the end of the line is on the right. There were similar ramps at other stations. (A.W.V.Mace/Milepost 92½)

18.   We are back within sight of the main line building on 28th July 1952 in the presence of *Countess*. The structure was still standing in 2009, but containing retail units, formerly known as shops. (P.Q.Treloar)

19.   The shunter is between the wagons as no. 822 stands in Smithfield Road. The line in the foreground leads to the transhipment shed. (L.M.Hobdey/J.M.Bentley coll.)

20.   *Countess* runs between the yards, the local goods shed being on the left. The locomotive retains its steam heating pipe, but without the hose. Steam heating was not required after passenger operations ceased. (A.J.B.Dodd/P.Chancellor coll.)

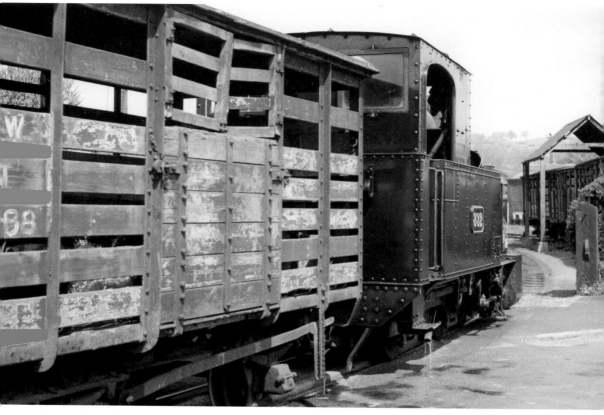

21.   Seen from the same crossing on 17th May 1956 is *The Earl* with a decaying cattle wagon. Others seek shelter near the goods shed, by then little used. (H.Davies)

22.　　Still with its obligatory lamp in place, no. 823 pauses upon arrival from Llanfair. The point levers are weighted to avoid blade vibration. (R.H.G.Simpson/P.Q.Treloar coll.)

23.　　The end is nigh as no. 822 stands before the camera on 30th June 1956. The track was ageing, with only five out of eight fishplate bolts present. The last day of steam on the main line was 4th March 1967. (G.Adams/M.J.Stretton coll.)

24.　　　Closure had taken place and the yard was a sorry sight on 7th September 1957. The rolling stock sheds are on the left. The locomotives were in Oswestry Works; *The Earl* returned in 1961 followed by *The Countess* in 1962. (M.Dart)

Welshpool & Llanfair Light
Railway Preservation Co. Ltd.
ADULT RETURN
WELSHPOOL AND
LLANFAIR
AND BACK
Issued subject to the Company's
regulations and notices.
NOT TRANSFERABLE.
Williamson, Ticket Printer, Ashton

3725　WPL　LLA　3725

25.   By the time the cameras arrived on 6th April 1963, most of the track in the yard had been lifted and only the carriage shed remained standing. The general public was not conveyed. Unorthodox watering was required that day for the engine, which is no. 822 *The Earl*. The water column had been outside the engine shed, but a hose had to be used that day. (P.Chancellor coll.)

26.   A view of the rear of the train shows the ex-Admiralty 'Combination Car'. The headlight, rear light, tail lamp and klaxon are all evident. This coach had a short life on the line as it was dismantled in 1989. (Ted Hancock Books)

North of the Terminus

27.　　The first section of track with a field boundary was to be found on leaving Welshpool yard. Here a train is seen arriving from Llanfair on 24th August 1948. The steam in the background is from a locomotive on the main line. (H.C.Casserley)

28.   A 1951 record features no. 822 a little further north on the severe 1 in 33 climb to the canal bridge. The goods mix is typical for the period. (P.Q.Treloar coll.)

29.   No. 823 has reached the bridge over the canal on 11th May 1949 with sheeted wagons from Llanfair. The crew can now relax. (M.Whitehouse coll.)

30. It is 31st March 1953 and youths observe some of the heating supplies for the homes of Llanfair passing over the canal, under the care of no. 822. (J.A.Peden/P.Q.Treloar coll.)

31. The Montgomeryshire Canal had been completed to Newtown in 1821 and it transformed the commerce and prosperity of the district. The worn ground suggests that this was a popular footbridge; it is now an official one. (P.Chancellor coll.)

32. A bad image, but a good opportunity to record a rare steaming of both engines. It is probably the members special train of August 1963. (M.Dart coll.)

Through the Town

Standard Quarry

Quarry Disused

Rock Cottages

Pump

Spring

Spring

W.M.

B R O O K

Ward Bdy

Brewery

Corn Mill

Allotment Gardens

Lledan Brook F.P.

R.C. Church

Clifton Street

F. Bs.

F. B.

M

Raven Square

Weir

F. B.

S

RAVEN STREET

MOUNT

P.H.

P.H.

Raven Bridge

33.   A pre-1931 postcard record of Church Street includes the charm of a kerbside petrol pump, no doubt hand cranked. Some of the buildings on the other side of the line from the photographer were demolished to provide an entrance to Brook Street so that traffic could bypass the main street. (P.Q.Treloar coll.)

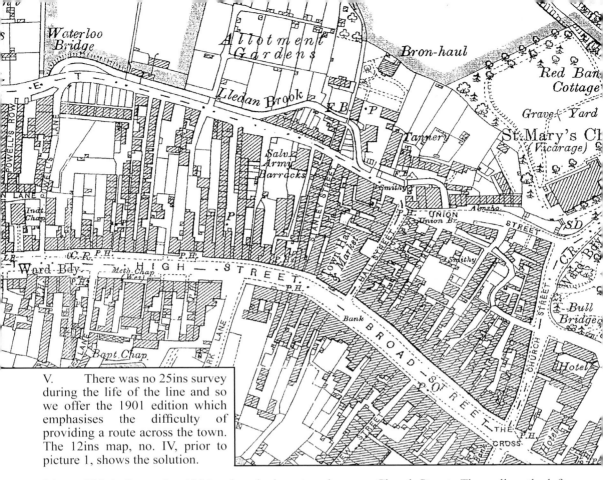

V.   There was no 25ins survey during the life of the line and so we offer the 1901 edition which emphasises the difficulty of providing a route across the town. The 12ins map, no. IV, prior to picture 1, shows the solution.

34.   This is September 1956 and we look eastwards across Church Street. The wall on the left had been repositioned for the railway. It formed the southern boundary of the vicarage, marked *Vic* on map IV. (M.Dart)

35.   The guard's view on 24th August 1948 includes many empty wagons on the 2.15pm from Llanfair. Some washing is obvious, while other items dry on a window cill. The loco is crossing Church Street. (H.C.Casserley)

CAMBRIAN RAILWAYS
Issued subject to the conditions
stated on the Co's Time Tables.
Welshpool(SevenStars) To
LLANFAIR CAEREINION
FIRST CLASS   FARE 1/3.
Welshpool(S.S)   Welshpool(S.S)
LlanfairCaereinion   LlanfairCaereinion

MY 12 08   405

CAM. RYS. Return
PRIVILEGE TICKET
Available for One Mon'
from date of issue
LlanfairCaereinio'
TO
WELSHPOOL(S.Stars
THIRD CLASS
Not   (F
Transferable   Lli

8811

36.   Shoppers have a rare treat as *The Countess* passes over Church Street on 6th April 1963 with the train seen in pictures 25 and 26. (P.Q.Treloar coll.)

VI. The most complex part of the route was where there were already two road bridges over Lledan Brook. (Railway Magazine)

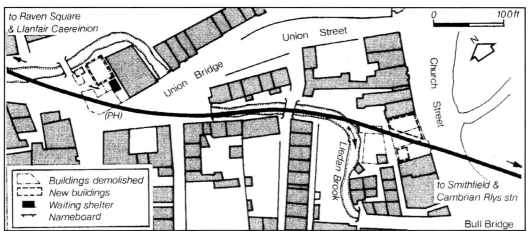

to Raven Square
& Llanfair Caereinion

Union Street

0   100ft

N

Union Bridge

Church Street

(PH)

Lledan Brook

Buildings demolished
New buildings
Waiting shelter
Nameboard

to Smithfield &
Cambrian Rlys stn

Bull Bridge

37.   It is June 1968 and this is the commencement of the section built on girders spanning the Lledan Brook. This technique reduced the amount of demolition required. There is a level crossing in the centre of the picture. (C.L.Caddy)

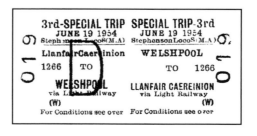

38.   No. 823 is bound for Llanfair on 28th July 1952. The level crossing is in the foreground and it had almost zero visibility. (P.Q.Treloar)

39.　　A few yards further on and we examine the location in more detail on 14th September 1953. Note the seating provided; it came from Welshpool station waiting room. (D.T.Rowe)

40.   A clearer view was obtained on 16th September 1948 of the family bath and garments drying on the line and railings. This is the west end of 'The Narrows' where the railway is above Lledan Brook. Shortly the train will emerge to cross the end of Union Street. (J.H.Meredith)

41.   On 4th June 1953, we witness no. 822 with a train from Llanfair. A parked car has to be removed before proceeding further along Union Street. The Coronation decorations are on the left. (Millbrook House)

42.   A different aspect of St. Mary's Church appears in both this and the next picture.   An early postcard includes the ventilators of a passenger coach outlined, plus an overtype steam wagon.
(P.Q.Treloar coll.)

43.   Slightly further towards Llanfair we enjoy a long freight train at an earlier date, before yellow lines had been invented. Seven Stars Halt had been to the left of the camera. It was provided with a waiting room, which later became the premises of an undertaker. (SLS coll.)

44.   At the site of the Seven Stars Halt our goods train, comprising empty wagons, proceeds from Llanfair towards its destination. On the left is a fine Wolseley 14 and two Austins are on the right. (A.W.V.Mace/Milepost 92½)

45.   Leaving on the 11.30 from Welshpool on 14th September 1956, no. 822 passes a life expired Austin 14 from the late-1930s. The train is running from Brook Street into Bron-y-Buckley. (R.M.Casserley)

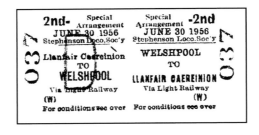

46. A policeman is at the ready as a special train runs down the 1 in 30 gradient across the entrance of Nelson Place. It is the train seen in picture 25 returning. (Ted Hancock Books)

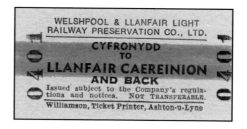

47.   The line climbed 100ft in under one mile and was subject to a 5mph speed limit through the urban part. The gradient in this area was 1 in 51 and 1 in 40. (R.M.Casserley)

48.   Houses in Bron-y-Buckley have back gardens adjacent to the line in the town, as witnessed from the 2.15pm from Llanfair on 24th August 1948. (H.C.Casserley)

Raven Square Halt

49.   The nameboard is on the left in the view looking towards the town. In the background is the Standard Quarry. This quarry had a siding until 1939 and is in the background. The halt had no shelter. (R.M.Casserley coll.)

50.   No. 822 has passed over the simple road junctions which are devoid of kerbs. The date is 24th August 1948. The brake van is across the A490, the road to Guilsfield, before the roundabout was built. (H.C.Casserley)

51.   The kerbs associated with the new roundabout are evident on 19th August 1952 as no. 822 climbs across the A490 on its journey to Llanfair. The locomotive nameplates were removed in 1950. (W.A.Camwell/SLS coll.)

52.   This SLS trip ran on 3rd November 1956 and *The Earl* is seen leaving the site of the halt after a stop for photography. (D.Luscombe/SLS coll.)

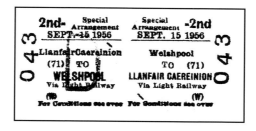

WELSHPOOL RAVEN SQUARE

53.   The first notable event at the new station was the appearance of *The Countess* on 19th July 1986, after a prolonged period of surgery. She is piloting no. 14 on the 5.15pm departure, while diesel 0-6-0 *Chattenden* stands on the right. (H.Ballantyne)

VII.   The 1982 plan for the new station includes the diversion of the Sylfaen Brook. Traffic commenced on 18th July 1981. A siding had been laid here in 1960 and it became a loop in 1964, but was little used. (Railway Magazine)

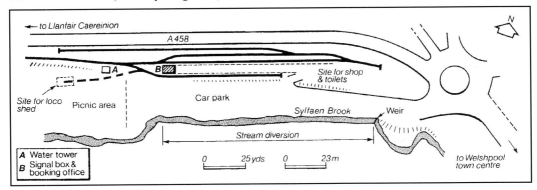

54. The signalbox had been completed for the opening of the new station. This view was taken on 24th May 1987. The LNWR lever frame came from Groeslon, on the line between Caernarfon and Afonwen. No.14 is pleasing the photographers. (T.Heavyside)

55. There were still no terminal buildings when this picture was taken on 12th July 1987. It was the "Steam Gala Day" and two cars served as the shop, while *Joan* was in the bay platform. The van in the distance served as the ticket office; the signal box lean-to in picture 54 was used at other times. (H.Ballantyne)

56.   No. 12 *Joan* is running in on 6th May 1991. The car park had been built on reclaimed marshland near the stream. The point (centre) was to serve an engine shed, which was never built. (T.Heavyside)

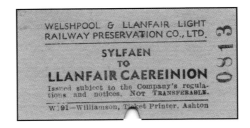

WELSHPOOL & LLANFAIR LIGHT
RAILWAY PRESERVATION CO., LTD.

SYLFAEN
TO
LLANFAIR CAEREINION

Issued subject to the Company's regulations and notices. NOT TRANSFERABLE.

W191—Williamson, Ticket Printer. Ashton

57.   No.7 *Chattenden* reverses past the signalbox on 9th August 1992. In the background is the severe gradient of 1 in 35, which trains have to tackle on their way to Llanfair. The original gradient through the present station site had been 1 in 58, but this was reduced to 'Level' when the present terminus was built. (P.G.Barnes)

→ 58. The building was completed in April 1992 and was based on a design used by the Hereford, Hay & Brecon Railway in 1861. The work was recorded in progress in November 1991. (R.I.Cartwright)

59.   *The Countess* had her original number restored and is posing with it on 12th September 1992 at the head of the 14.45 to Llanfair. A stylish ventilator adorns the smart new building. (T.Heavyside)

60.   Moving on to 2nd September 1995, we can enjoy *Countess* restored to GWR condition as no. 823, while the station shows its Welsh name. (T.Heavyside)

61.   No.19 is at the end of the line on 24th May 2008. The part of the building seen had formed the station at Eardisley; see pictures 38 to 40 in *Branch Lines around Hay-on-Wye*. The water tower was erected in 2001. It served its previous working life at Pwllheli. (H.Ballantyne)

WEST OF WELSHPOOL

62.   A popular postcard was produced to include Welshpool Reservoir, but probably not to emphasise the unusually irregular width of the sleepers. Maybe this was the contractor's temporary track.   This section is known as 'Glyn Golfa' and is at 1 in 54. The train is seen approaching the now closed Golfa Halt.   The halt once had a loop; its points were lifted in 1969 and 1997. (E.Jones/P.Q.Treloar coll.)

OPENING CEREMONY,

Saturday, 4th April, 1903.

OFFICIAL PROGRAMME.

11-13 a.m.—Special Train will leave Welshpool Station
  for Llanfair.

*(Free Railway Passes—not transferable—will be sent on
  application to all Shareholders of £15 and upwards).*

12-13 p.m.—Reception at Llanfair Station.

1-0 p.m.—Special Train leaves Llanfair.

1-43 p.m.—Special Train arrives at Welshpool.

2-0 p.m.—Public Luncheon at the Royal Oak Hotel,
  Welshpool.   Chairman : The Earl of Powis.
  Tickets, 3/6 each.

The Directors much regret that the small space at their disposal
obliges them to limit the issue of Free Railway Passes.

To ensure seats being reserved at the Luncheon Table, Tickets
should be taken at the Royal Oak Hotel, Welshpool, not later than
Tuesday, March 31st.

JOHN EVANS.

SECRETARY.

24, Broad Street, Welshpool,
  23rd March, 1903.

SYLFAEN

63. Sylfaen opened as "Sylfaen Farm Halt" but was renamed "Sylfaen" on 1st February 1913. Few people live nearby. The revived service from Llanfair was extended to this location on 6th June 1964, but no loop was provided. There was simply a siding and no.3 *Raven* provides the engine release loco on 18th July 1964. The service ran for exactly three months and did not resume until 15th July 1972. (C.G.Maggs)

VIII. Track diagram 1903-56, with later buildings. (J.C.Gillham)

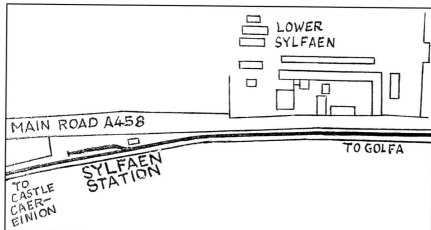

64.   No. 1 *The Earl* is about to return to Llanfair on 27th May 1973. To create a loop, additional land had to be purchased and its level raised substantially. (T.Heavyside)

65.   It was not until 1977 that the run round loop was available. The track was provided to a high standard. No.14 was recorded on 2nd June 1979. (T.Heavyside)

66.   The 15.00 from Welshpool had been double headed up the steep gradient on 24th May 1987. No. 2 is restarting the train, while no.14 waits to return to Welshpool. (T.Heavyside)

67.   The peaceful location was photographed on 24th May 2008 as 0-8-0T no. 19 pauses briefly. This was a regular passing place in 1984-88. (H.Ballantyne)

WEST OF SYLFAEN

68.   No. 822 runs west after descending Sylfaen Bank on 24th August 1948. Eleven vans or wagons were the maximum permitted load. (H.C.Casserley)

69.   Users of Coppice Lane are protected by the flag held by the fireman on 27th May 1973, while the passengers enjoy the delights of Austrian travel. *The Earl* is in charge. Later, trains were allowed to whistle and cross the road without stopping. (T.Heavyside)

70.   At the same location on 6th May 1991 we observe bogie coaches from Sierra Leone hauled by no. 10 *Sir Drefaldwyn*. Austrian four wheeler are at the front and back. Sir means *Shire* and is usually pronounced *Sear*. (T.Heavyside)

71.   No. 822 is running towards Welshpool on 24th August 1948. Grass has taken over the yard on the left. Sheaves of corn dry in the lush fields, before the advent of combine harvesters. (H.C.Casserley)

IX. Track evolution. (J.C.Gillham)

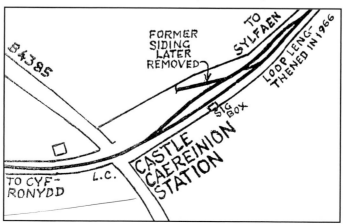

72.   The signal box dates from 1907, but served as a tool store for most of its life. Signals were provided, but never used regularly. (P.Q.Treloar coll.)

73.   Another undated view and this includes the waiting shelter for passengers, along with bench seats for excursionists. It was against the rules to carry passengers in unbraked stock! There had been a short siding behind no. 823. (P.Q.Treloar coll.)

74.   History was recorded in the presence of a band on 3rd November 1956 as no. 822 hauled what was expected to be the last train here. (C.L.Caddy)

75.   Much water had flowed down the brook before the next and happier occasion. There are smiles all round on 6th April 1963 when there was a regular train of passengers for the first time since 1931. (Ted Hancock Books)

76.   It is 2nd June 1968 and improved waiting facilities are evident. Services terminated here from 1965 to 1971 inclusive. (M.J.Stretton coll.)

77.   With drain cocks open, no.1 *The Earl* hisses away as it leaves for Llanfair on 27th May 1973, with a remarkably diverse rake of coaching stock. (T.Heavyside)

78.   No.12 *Joan* adds to the foreign ambiance presented on 19th August 1978, when it had two Austrian (Zillertalbahn) coaches and one Sierra Leone coach on a special. The Zillertalbahn is featured in the *Austrian Narrow Gauge* album. The building on the left represented a border customs post in the TV film *The Prisoner of Zenda*. (T.Heavyside)

79.   The second platform, added for the film mentioned, is evident as trains pass on 9th August 1992; pity about the car on it. *The Countess* is about to leave for Llanfair. (P.G.Barnes)

80.   The entrance to the new platform is on the left and a level crossing gate is on the right in this 1993 view. The signal box housed radio equipment from 1994, this allowing communication with the trains, blockposts and persons working on the line. (B.W.L.Brooksbank)

CYFRONYDD

81.   A postcard view eastwards from around 1930 features the standard shelter, but does not include the cattle dock and timber loading crane, which were later additions. (SLS coll.)

82   A 1956 photograph confirms that the siding was used mostly for wagon storage by that time. On the running line is the petrol trolley used by the ganger. Cyfronydd is pronounced "kuv-ron-ith". (H.Ballantyne)

X. Track plan since 1996. (J.C.Gillham)

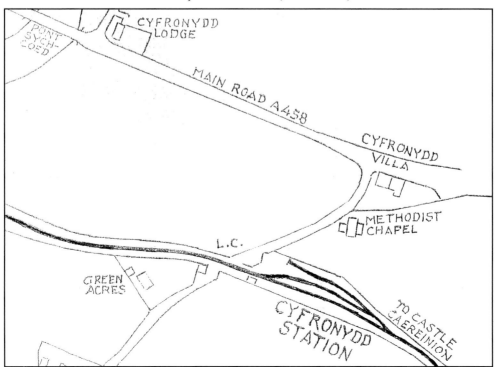

83. No.14 runs in with the 12.15 from Welshpool on 19th July 1986, as no. 2 waits with a single coach to take the Carnival Queen into Llanfair in style. There was a siding in 1967-80 and again from 1996.
(H.Ballantyne)

84. The loop became a passing place in 1995 and on 2nd September of that year accommodated 0-6-0WT no. 105. This Henschel was a Gala Weekend visitor from the Bredgar & Wormshill Railway, which is featured in our *Kent Narrow Gauge* album.
(T.Heavyside)

WEST OF
CYFRONYDD

85.　　The growth of vegetation deprived
visitors of a view of this elegant structure,
part of which is glimpsed on 3rd June 1968,
as *The Earl* proceeds with the 1.25pm from
Castle Caereinion. (H.Ballantyne)

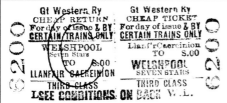

86.　　Seen in 1948, the superstructure
of Brynelin Viaduct stands on six 25ft
arches and the total length is 50 yards.
(J.H.Meredith)

← 87. A goods train was assembled for photographic purposes on 1st April 2000 and *The Earl* was photographed to good advantage on the historic structure. The viaduct spans a small valley which sometimes contains a rivulet flowing into the River Banwy. It is called the Brynelyn Brook. (M.Turvey)

← 88. *The Earl* pauses on the Banwy Bridge, which is one mile further west. The train is the LCGB "Summer Tour" special on 23rd June 1956. The three spans total 114 feet in length. (I.Gammell/P.Q.Treloar coll.)

89. The western pier foundations were eroded by fierce floodwater on 13th December 1964 and this displacement followed. The entire railway revival project was in jeopardy. (W&LLR Pres. Co.)

90.   The enterprise of many involved resulted in the Army offering to erect this temporary support and the future of the railway was secured. This and the next photograph date from 14th July 1965. (C.L.Caddy)

91.   The occasion gave an opportunity to examine the internal bracing. The undisturbed third span is in the distance. (C.L.Caddy)

92.   The steel pier is seen on 31st August 1991 as *The Countess* passes over with the 14.55 from Llanfair. The steelwork was encased in concrete following further erosion of the base in 1997 and it was faced with stone. (H.Ballantyne)

HENIARTH

93.　　No. 822 *The Earl* was recorded at the grass covered location with the 12 noon from Welshpool on 24th August 1948. A single timber bolster is seen in the siding. The station was originally called "Heniarth Gate", but was renamed on 1st February 1913. (H.C.Casserley)

XI. 1965 track diagram. (J.C.Gillham)

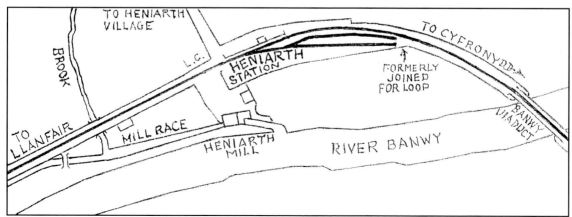

94.   The same locomotive is seen on the return journey that day. Both bolsters are apparent. These were used with a flat wagon between them for carrying long loads such as tree trunks. (H.C.Casserley)

95.   A healthy traffic was to be seen on 5th September 1950 as *The Countess* crept up the 1 in 160 towards Llanfair. The maximum length train is seen. (P.Q.Treloar coll.)

96.   Our survey continues with three photographs from 6th April 1963. Here is the main entrance, in the ultimate tranquil setting. (A.M.Davies)

CAMBRIAN RAILWAYS.
Issued subject to the Conditions
stated in the Co's Time Tables.
Llanfair Caereinion to
HENIARTH GATE
THIRD CLASS PARLY   FARE ═/1½
Llanfair Caereinion   Llanfair Caereinion
HeniarthGate   HeniarthGate

97.   An historic moment was recorded as the "Reopening Special" ran through. Stock was stored in the siding, owing to congestion at Llanfair. The sidings had gone by 1979. (A.M.Davies)

98.   The special is returning and is photographed passing Dolrhyd Mill on its way to Heniarth. The track was in an unrestored condition with little more than 'rough gardening' having been undertaken. (A.M.Davies)

99.   Moving to more recent times, we witness 2-6-2T no.14 with a further variety of stock on 28th August 1999. There is little evidence of the former siding. (H.Ballantyne)

WEST OF HENIARTH

100.   The entire working carriage stock was a rare sight and is captured on this early postcard view (pre-1931) at Melindolrhydydefaid (Dolrhyd Mill). (P.Q.Treloar coll.)

EAST OF LLANFAIR CAEREINION

101. Nostrils emerge as the train stops for water on 16th September 1948. The tank was close to the River Banwy, but was not used after 1979, when a mains supply was provided at Llanfair. The pump is at the bottom of the tank support right legs and its operating handle projects from the large wheel above. (J.H.Meredith)

102. The SLS tour on 30th June 1956 paused for refreshment for no. 822, by then devoid of its nameplate. It had left Llanfair at 11.20. (H.C.Casserley)

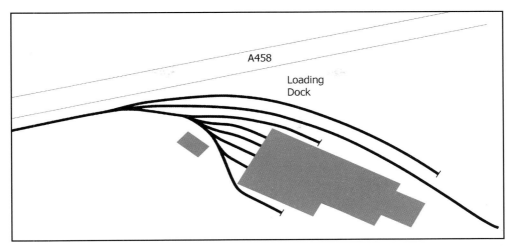

XII.   Tanllan Siding was laid down originally for timber traffic. It is the one north of the running line, but the point was at its other end. A nearby level site proved suitable for a carriage shed and workshop. (E.Pede)

103.   The spacious carriage shed was nearing completion in April 1989 and it would later be fitted out with a range of woodworking machinery. The first of three carriage sidings had been laid here in 1975. (R.I.Cartright)

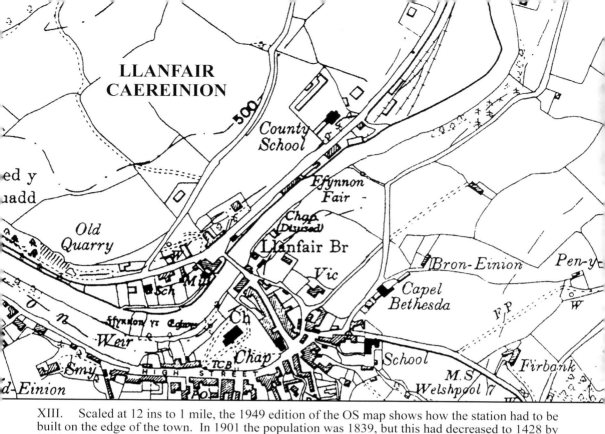

XIII. Scaled at 12 ins to 1 mile, the 1949 edition of the OS map shows how the station had to be built on the edge of the town. In 1901 the population was 1839, but this had decreased to 1428 by 1961. In the 2001 census the population was 1616.

104. Train crew, station staff and two trackmen probably make up the group posing for the photographer soon after the opening. There is no smoke from *The Earl*, but there is from the brake van. (P.J.Kelley coll.)

105.   *The Earl* is prominent again and is attached to two carriages. The first is a 'composite' with the first class section seating 10 people at the rear and 26 third class seats at the front. A guards compartment containing a brake wheel was provided in the centre. The other carriage is all third class with 46 seats. (P.Q.Treloar coll.)

106.   The GWR listed a staff of three here in 1923. In the early years there was a booking office, but later all tickets were issued on the train. All operating employees were based at Welshpool. *The Earl* is seen on 9th July 1925 bearing the GWR number 822. (R.M.Casserley coll.)

107.   The platform was provided for the benefit of livestock and not passengers. It is apparent that it was also used for farm equipment and direct access to the main road is evident. The huts were offices for the coal merchants and beyond the cattle wagon is the road to the yard. (H.C.Casserley)

108.   Turning round on 24th August 1948, we witness no. 822 running round its train. The office canopy seen in picture 104 had gone, but accommodation had been increased by the provision of a mainline coach body on blocks. (H.C.Casserley)

109.   Seen on arrival is the SLS special on 30th June 1956, complete with a bench in the wagon. Two coal merchants used part of the yard and such business continued until 1972. There was a 2 ton crane available for many years.
(H.C.Casserley)

110.   No. 822 is standing on the points after running in with the LCGB farewell train on 23rd June 1956. The coal in the foreground was for local use and not for the locomotives. (P.Q.Treloar coll.)

→ 111. *The Earl* is about to depart on 4th August 1965, while *The Countess* stands at the end of the line. Nearest is the ex-Admiralty Combination Car, no. 214. The term "Composite" was used on most railways. The body went to the South Tynedale Railway in 1989 and later to the Welsh Highland. (R.A.Lumber/D.H.Mitchell coll.)

→   112.   *The Countess* is being prepared for service on 11th August 1968, while *The Earl* waits behind it. The signalbox contains a frame which came from Llanbrynmair in 1967. (C.L.Caddy)

Llanfair Caereinion	1923
Passenger tickets issued	9438
Season tickets issued	7
Parcels forwarded	5492
General goods forwarded (tons)	712
Coal and coke received (tons)	2776
Other minerals received (tons)	2749
General goods received (tons)	2458
Trucks of livestock handled	294

113.   A panorama from September 1968 includes all the old buildings, plus one intruder. The goods shed shelter on the left was the only protection for locomotives until 1971. (B.W.L.Brooksbank)

XIV. Track diagram for 1975. (J.C.Gillham)

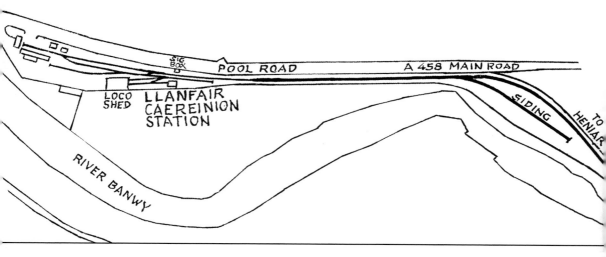

114.   No. 5 *Nutty* was photographed on 22nd June 1968; it was on the line until October 1971. It was built at the Sentinel Waggon Works in Shrewsbury and fitted with one of its famous water tube vertical boilers, twin cylinders and chain drive. It was built for 2ft 11ins gauge and has its chimney close to the whistle. The boiler is in the cab and there is a cranked flue. (C.L.Caddy)

115.   On display on 19th August 1978 was another low profile locomotive, no.8 *Dougal*, built by Andrew Barclay & Sons Ltd for restricted confines. On the left is no.10 *Sir Drefaldwyn* and on the right is no.14. The journey home of no.14 is illustrated in the final eight photographs in *Sierra Leone Narrow Gauge*. On its journey it was accompanied by four coaches. (T.Heavyside)

116. "Little and Large" on 30th June 1979. The monster no. 6 *Monarch* has Meyer type power bogies and a long marine boiler. This locomotive proved unsuitable for the steep gradients of the line and departed in 1992. It returned to be restored as a static exhibit in 2002. The smaller locomotive is no. 8 *Dougal*. (F.Hornby)

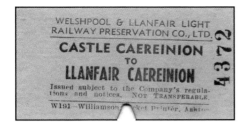

117.   No. 14 runs in on 2nd June 1979 and we can admire the rebuilt signal box. Its replacement can be seen in the next picture. (T.Heavyside)

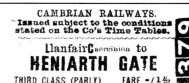

CAMBRIAN RAILWAYS.
Issued subject to the conditions
stated on the Co's Time Tables.
LlanfairCaereinion to
HENIARTH GATE
THIRD CLASS (PARLY)   FARE -/1½
4379
LlanfairCaereinion   LlanfairCaereinion
HeniarthGate   HeniarthGate

118.   Arriving in 2007 was this Resita-built 0-8-0T, no.19. Another, no. 18, had arrived three years earlier. Others of this type can be seen in the first section of the *Romania & Bulgaria Narrow Gauge* album. The new signal box, seen here, was erected in 2001. (M.J.Stretton)

119.   The final pictures are from 25th June 2008. Nearest is no. 7 *Chattenden*, which spent the first part of its Naval career on the Lodge Hill & Upnor Railway. This is included in our *Kent Narrow Gauge* album. No. 17 was built by Diema and had only been on the line for four years. (Mrs J.A.Smith)

↘120. The end of the line has the unusual feature of a removable bridge. The original buildings each side have been commendably restored and the entrance was moved to the left in 1980. The 2000 building in the right background includes toilets deserving high praise. (Mrs J.A.Smith)

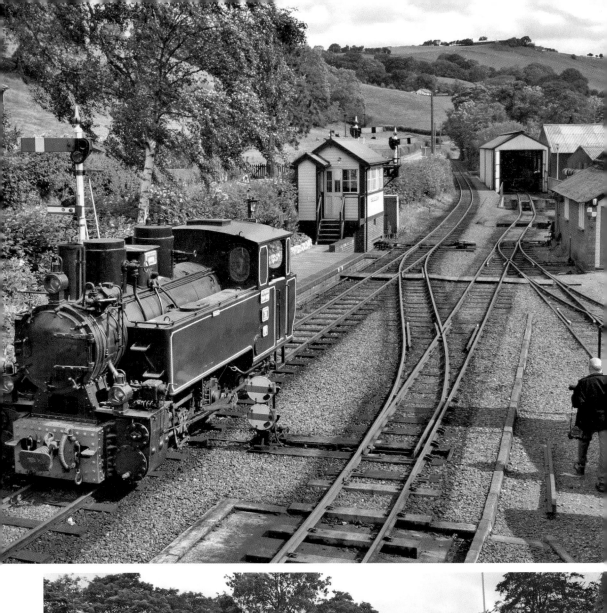

MP Middleton Press
EVOLVING THE ULTIMATE RAIL ENCYCLOPEDIA

Easebourne Lane, Midhurst, West Sussex.
GU29 9AZ   Tel:01730 813169

www.middletonpress.co.uk   email:info@middletonpress.co.uk
A-978 0 906520 B- 978 1 873793 C- 978 1 901706 D-978 1 904474 E- 978 1 906008

OOP Out of print at time of printing - Please check availability   BROCHURE AVAILABLE SHOWING NEW TITLES